Algrove Publishing Limited
1090 Morrison Drive
Ottawa, Ontario
Canada K2H 1C2

Canadian Cataloguing in Publication Data

Powell, F. E.
    Windmills and wind motors : how to build and run them

(Classic reprint series)
Reprint of the ed. published: New York : Spon & Chamberlain,
1918. First published 1910.
ISBN 0-921335-84-9

    1. Windmills. 2. Wind power. I. Title. II. Series: Classic
reprint series (Ottawa, Ont.)

TJ825.P69 1999   621.4'53   C99-900864-1

Printed in Canada
#30600

Publisher's Note

There is a joy in reprinting a book of this type that is totally unrelated to the expected economic gain. It is a pleasure to be able to put a book on the market that provides so much arcane information in such an enthusiastic manner. The author easily achieves his aim "...to present a series of practical original designs that should prove useful to every reader from the youngest to the most advanced."

Whether your interest is in making a simple anemometer or a pantanemone (a precursor to the modern turbine), the author covers a range that will let you engage the subject at any level you wish, from simple models to actual working windmills. It shows the confidence of a century ago that the only thing preventing people from achieving their aspirations was want of information and application. It is a delightful book.

Leonard G. Lee, Publisher
Ottawa
September, 1999

WINDMILLS

AND

WIND MOTORS

HOW TO
BUILD AND RUN THEM

BY

F. E. POWELL

FULLY ILLUSTRATED WITH DETAIL DRAWINGS

NEW YORK
SPON & CHAMBERLAIN
120-122 LIBERTY STREET
1918

(No. 36.)

CAMELOT PRESS, 226-228 WILLIAM ST., NEW YORK, U. S. A.

PREFACE

I have endeavoured in the following pages not only to interest the practical amateur in a branch of mechanics unfortunately much neglected, but also to present a series of practical original designs that should prove useful to every reader from the youngest to the most advanced. This is admittedly a large undertaking, and would be of doubtful wisdom, but for the sparseness of the literature of the subject. There is, however, no other book in the language, large or small, dealing with the matter in the way here presented, and indeed only one other, as far as I know, having the subject of windmills for its sole topic. I venture to hope therefore that this little book will help to arouse something of the interest the subject deserves but has not hitherto received.

That I am right in claiming for the wind motor a more serious recognition I am convinced, and particularly is this the case in regard to the model engineer. At present there is every prejudice against wind-power on account of its uncertainty, against which even its inexpensiveness has not been able to contend.

If it can once be realised, however, that the uncertainty can be reduced to little or no importance, so much that even a petrol-engine might seem unreliable and troublesome beside it, the claim put forward for the windmill is fully substantiated. Not less than this is one of the aims of this little book, and it is one which I confidently expect will be upheld.

In a book like this, trenching upon new ground, where every design has been the outcome of careful consideration unaided by the experience of others, it is not unlikely that errors or ambiguities may have crept in. The reader who finds any such, or who meets with difficulties of any sort, will confer a kindness by communicating them to the author through the publishers.

F. E. POWELL.

CONTENTS

CHAPTER IV

A SMALL WORKING WINDMILL

CHAPTER V

A PRACTICAL WORKING WINDMILL

CHAPTER VI

PRODUCTION OF ELECTRICITY BY WIND-POWER

CHAPTER I

Windmill Evolution

It is not a little strange that amateur engineers should have so neglected the windmill, either as a subject for model-making and experiment, or even for the more practical purpose of power production. Wind-power is free, and while it is admittedly erratic it must surely appeal to the mechanical mind as a labour saver of some value. The probability is that the lack of simple published designs is the main reason for this state of things, and the aim of this little book is to remedy it.

Few mechanical appliances have a simpler historical record than the windmill. Until comparatively recent years only two main types of mill were commonly in use, known respectively as the Post and the Tower mills. The former, which is the earlier machine, was distinguished by the fact that the whole building, carrying sails, house, cap, and all machinery, was pivoted on a huge timber post, so that the whole structure had to be removed when it was necessary to adjust the mill to face the wind. The Tower mill, called also the "Smock" and sometimes the "Frock" mill, was an improvement on the

other in having the cap only to revolve, carrying
with it the sails and (later) the automatic regulating mechanism for bringing the sails round

Fig. 1.—Ancient Post Mill: from an Old Mill at
Bornholm, Denmark.

"into the wind." Illustrations of these two
types of mills are given in figs. 1 and 2.

As hinted above, the automatic method of controlling the mill so that the sails should face the
wind was a fairly recent innovation. It dates
back to the middle of the eighteenth century,

when Andrew Meikle introduced the now well-known auxiliary regulating wheel, which may be seen in fig. 3

FIG. 2.—Tower Mill: at Hilleröd, Denmark.

Another advance in windmill construction was made in 1807, when Sir W. Cubitt introduced an automatic reefing arrangement for the sails. Be-

fore that date speed was more or less outside
the control of the operator, who could only throw
in or out his machinery as the speed ranged too

FIG. 3.—Tower Mill with Regulating or Wind Wheel.

high or too low, or by the application of brakes
could keep it partly within bounds.

The later history of the development of windmills must be looked for abroad. The inventor
of the "American" mill is said to have been
John Burnham, whose location is sufficiently in-

dicated in the name by which this type is known. The date was about the middle of the nineteenth century. Everyone knows that the distinction between the older types and the modern transatlantic machines lies in the number and disposition of the sails, which in the latter are numerous and form a comparatively narrow ring of vanes. A modern example of such a mill is illustrated in fig. 4. Since Burnham's day inventors have not been asleep, and the multitude of so-called American mills now on the market is evidence of their skill. These machines vary, however, only in details of design, regulation, and control, not in any essential character.

The American mill, though not much more efficient than its older competitor, has the advantages of cheapness, a more even turning movement, and easier starting. The defects, especially in the matter of economy, of all types of windmills led to a very remarkable series of experiments which were carried out by the Danish Government from 1891 until the death of the chief investigator, Prof. Poul la Cour, in 1908, brought them to an end. The work done by this enthusiastic engineer included not only the improvement of windmill details, but also a practical inquiry into the possibility of utilising wind-power in the production of electrical energy. Much of the collected data is naturally negative in its results, but students of the subject must always look with warm admiration on

the patient work of La Cour and the good sense
of the State that assisted him

As far as this book is concerned, the Danish

FIG. 4.—Modern Type of Windmill.

experiments have one special bearing. They
proved that for maximum *power* and speed the
modern multi-sailed machines could not com-

pete with a four- or six-armed mill of modified design. This type is comparatively easy to construct in a modified form, and has so many advantages that one or two designs in the following pages have been based upon it.

.   .   .   .   .   .

Besides the standard types of windmills previously mentioned, many other wind motors

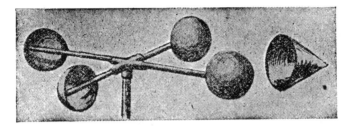

FIG. 5.
Diagram of Anemometer.

FIG. 6.
Alternative Cups.

have been suggested and used at times, and deserve at least brief notice. One of the simplest of these is the ordinary anemometer used for measurement of wind velocities (see fig. 5). It consists of four hemispherical cups carried on cross-arms, which are pivoted at their junction and moved by the superior resistance offered by the concavity of any one of the cups facing the wind. It will of course start in a wind of any direction whatever in the plane of its revolution, but has no pretension to power production. The hemispheres may be replaced by small (tin) cones (fig. 6), which are more easily made.

Another windmill of extreme simplicity, which has sometimes been made of a large size, illustrated in fig. 7, is called a " Jumbo." The small illustration in the corner of fig. 7 is a diagram-

FIG. 7.—" Jumbo," or Horizontal Windmill.

matic end view of this type of motor. Arrows show the direction of wind and of rotation. The action is sufficiently indicated in the sketch, and it need only be pointed out that the great disadvantage is that it will only work with certain winds. It is also necessary to have a large open space free from trees or buildings if the best results are looked for.

A modified form of the last machine is that shown in fig. 8, which has four or more sails mounted on a vertical shaft and arranged with a semicircular shield which runs on a circular path so that the vanes can be acted upon by the wind on one side only. Obviously the advantage in

FIG. 8.—Wind Motor with Vertical Axle.

this case is that winds of any direction can be made to perform work, but the type has never been developed to any extent.

Another wind motor worth illustrating is, however, rather more curious than useful. This is the pantanemone, shown in fig. 9. It consists simply of two semicircular discs whose diameters are placed at right angles to one another, the shaft being between them, in the same plane as the diameters, but at 45° to each of them.

The amater may be interested to make a model on these lines, which, while without practical value, is interesting for the fact that the machine will start in wind of any direction.

Other wind motors there are, of varying inter-

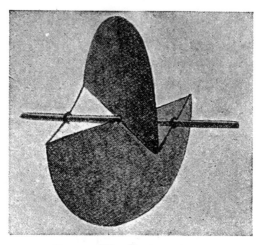

Fig. 9.—The Pantanemone.

est and usefulness, including a quite modern development on the lines of a turbine, which has not yet seen the light of a manufacturer's workshop. Space, however, is too valuable to be given to any but well-tried designs, although much interesting experimental work remains to be done in this connection on systematic lines.

CHAPTER II

A Small Working Model Windmill. Tower Mill Type

Considering the simplicity of a windmill model and the fact that it will not easily get out of order, it is surprising that more amateurs do not turn their hands to its construction. A windmill with sails of only 2 feet diameter, such as will now be described, will develop in even a moderate breeze fully as much power as an average steam-engine with cylinder say 1 inch stroke by ¾-inch diameter, and will therefore be quite powerful enough to drive a model workshop, work a model crane, or do other similar light work. An interesting combination suitable for outdoors, where of course the windmill must work, would be a model railway arranged on an incline so that by means of a long cord the mill might be made to draw up a train to the top of the slope, the descent being made by gravity. This is not the place to enter into details, which nevertheless would not be very abstruse and would form an interesting problem to be carried out by the young mechanic.

Too much importance should not be attached to the idea that wind is unreliable as a motive force. It will be found more reliable than is usually supposed, and apart from that the simplicity of construction, in which no lathe and very few tools are required, as well as the absence of cost in working, should all go to make the model windmill a popular object.

The design shown in fig. 10 is for a model of the size already mentioned, namely, with sails 24 inches across the tips. It will be of course quite easy for the reader to make his model either larger or smaller, if he so desires, by taking care to increase or decrease the dimensions of all parts in proportion. In a model like this it would only be introducing unnecessary complication if any attempt were made to provide the adjustments usual in large mills, and indeed it is quite possible that such regulating gear would take all the available power of the machine to work it. The design therefore dispenses with any such elaborations, but the maker can, if so disposed, and without any great difficulty, arrange for the top of the mill to turn automatically, so that the sails always face the wind. A study of the later chapters of this book will show how this can be done.

Almost all the materials used in the construction are cardboard and wood, so that the model is not intended to be left permanently out in all weathers. If this should be desired, a larger use of wood must be made, and tin or sheet-iron well painted should also enter into the construc-

FIG. 10   A Small Working Model Windmill.

tion. The baseboard in any case should be a substantial bit of timber, weighted if necessary, or otherwise, well secured to avoid overturning in a strong breeze.

The main part of tower is formed of stout cardboard, which should be well varnished after erection. It is cut out as shown in fig. 12, and slight cuts along the division lines will enable the eight sides to be formed up. A strip of stout paper glued inside and outside will complete the joint. Note that the outside strips should be cut very neatly and all the same widths. They will then take the appearance of the finishing boards usually fitted at the corners of a wooden building. While still in the flat, the various windows, doors, etc., should be pencilled firmly on the different sides, and particular care taken to fix any fitments for crane or other details. The whole model can be made very realistic if some little time is spent in lining out the tower and cap to represent weather-boarding, or, if preferred, in the case of the tower, stone or brick. Pencil lines will be best, and colour may be put on to enhance the effect. Some idea of the effect to be aimed at is indicated in the lower part of fig. 11.

The top and base of tower will be octagonal in plan, as shown in sketches, fig. 13.

Details of the head or cap are given in fig. 14, which, together with fig. 11, will give a good idea of the manner of construction. Fig. 15 shows

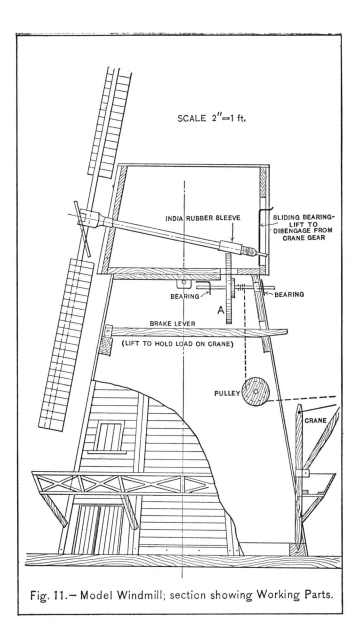

SCALE 2″=1 ft.

INDIA RUBBER SLEEVE

SLIDING BEARING-
LIFT TO
DISENGAGE FROM
CRANE GEAR

BEARING

BEARING

A

BRAKE LEVER

(LIFT TO HOLD LOAD ON CRANE)

PULLEY

CRANE

Fig. 11.— Model Windmill; section showing Working Parts.

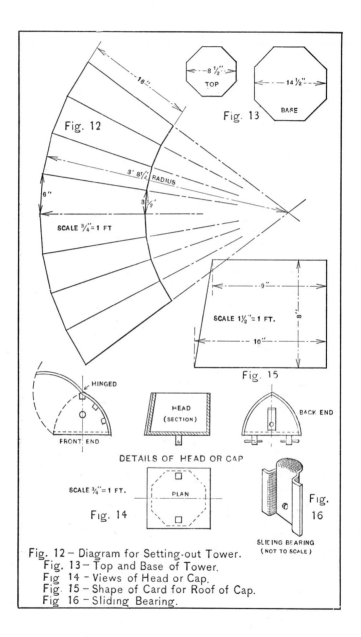

Fig. 12

16"

3' 8½" RADIUS

3½'

6"

SCALE ¾"= 1 FT

TOP
8½"

Fig. 13

BASE
14½"

9"

8"

10"

SCALE 1½"= 1 FT.

Fig. 15

HINGED

FRONT END

HEAD
(SECTION)

BACK END

DETAILS OF HEAD OR CAP

SCALE ¾"= 1 FT.

PLAN

Fig. 14

Fig. 16

SLIDING BEARING
(NOT TO SCALE)

Fig. 12 – Diagram for Setting-out Tower.
Fig. 13 – Top and Base of Tower.
Fig. 14 – Views of Head or Cap.
Fig. 15 – Shape of Card for Roof of Cap.
Fig. 16 – Sliding Bearing.

the shape of the two pieces of card to form the
roof of cap before bending to shape.

Pieces of cigar-box wood or thin pine form the
base and ends of cap, and should be joined by
very thin nails or stout pins, some deal sticks
about ½-inch square being used as spreaders or
stiffeners. The ends must be carefully set out
from centre lines, and holes nicely drilled and

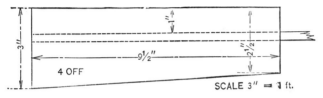

FIG. 17.—Shape of Sail for Model Windmill.

cut to the dimensions given. Their uses will be
apparent presently. One side of the roof should
be made to open with a hinge of calico to enable
the working parts to be got at.

Details of the arms and sails are given in figs.
17, 18, and 19, and readers unfamiliar with the
" setting" of windmill sails should carefully
study the drawings before shaping the arms.
As shown in fig. 18, the sails are not placed cen-
trally on the arm, which is much nearer one edge
than the other. This is shown in the sectional
view of arm and sail in fig. 18. Then also the
two sails on one arm point opposite ways, which
is perhaps best seen in the perspective sketch,

fig. 10. The amount by which the sail lies out of the plane of revolution is called its " angle of weather." To obtain this setting, each arm is bevelled away, the two ends being bevelled in opposite ways. Fig. 19 shows this, and the reader has only to imagine each arm brought successively into the same position, say the top, to realise how the bevel must always be the same way with the arm in that position. Fig. 20 will also be helpful in making this clear. A portion of the arm at its middle is left the full square section (see figs. 18 and 20, which show this). Every care must be taken to make the bevelling correctly, or one pair of sails would be found bevelled one way and the other in the opposite way. This would of course result in nullifying the effect of both. The axle, shown in various figures, especially 18, 21, and 22, is made of a piece of hard wood like oak or hickory, and is shaped specially to take the two arms as indicated in fig. 22. Care must be used not only to cut this out true and a good fit, but also not to break the thin prongs. The shaft must be nicely rounded and sand-papered smooth. At the collar portion, which will form the forward bearing, a little paraffin wax should be melted into the grain to reduce running friction, or, better still, a thin brass ferrule fitted, as shown in fig. 18.

The arms, in addition to being glued in place, must be further secured by wooden pins, and

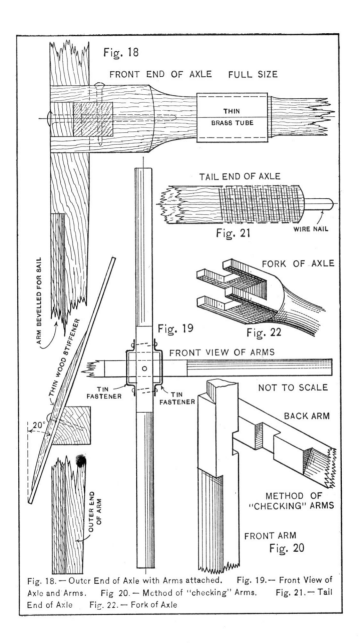

Fig. 18

FRONT END OF AXLE   FULL SIZE

THIN
BRASS TUBE

TAIL END OF AXLE

Fig. 21

WIRE NAIL

FORK OF AXLE

ARM BEVELLED FOR SAIL

THIN WOOD STIFFENER

Fig. 19

Fig. 22

FRONT VIEW OF ARMS

TIN
FASTENER

TIN
FASTENER

NOT TO SCALE

BACK ARM

20°

OUTER END OF ARM

METHOD OF
"CHECKING" ARMS

FRONT ARM
Fig. 20

Fig. 18.— Outer End of Axle with Arms attached.   Fig. 19.— Front View of
Axle and Arms.   Fig 20.— Method of "checking" Arms.   Fig. 21.— Tail
End of Axle   Fig. 22.— Fork of Axle

every care must be taken not only to fit them
correctly according to the bevels, but also to
get them dead square with the shaft and with
each other. The use of an ordinary set-square
will accomplish this. Both arms, as shown in
fig. 22, are slightly " checked " or " halved " into
each other, both to lock them more securely and
to reduce the overhang of shaft. Notice should
be taken that the cutaway is in the back of front
arm and front of rear arm.

The sails should be both glued and pinned to
the arms for security and a pencil line at the
right place on back of each sail will ensure get-
ting them correctly placed. Each sail, previous
to being mounted, should have parallel lines,
about half an inch apart, drawn across both faces
to imitate the slats generally used in large mills
of this type. After mounting, and when glue is
firm, the sails and outer ends of shaft should
have a couple of coats of good thin varnish to
enable them to stand some weather.

It may here be remarked that when pins are
used instead of nails they will be found much
easier to drive if a quarter of an inch of the sharp
point is nipped off. If this is not done, they are
almost sure to bend.

It will be seen that the tail end of shaft is provided with a metal bearing or journal in the form
of a small headless nail. This must be let in by
first very carefully boring an axial hole in shaft,
preferably with a twist drill, the end of shaft

being bound round to avoid splitting. This journal runs in a tin bearing (fig. 16), which is made to slide stiffly up and down in the slot in back of cap. This allows the owner to put in or out of gear the winding shaft by means of which the mill is caused to perform useful work. This is accomplished through the disc A, fig. 11, fixed on the winding shaft, a rubber band in circumference of disc and thin rubber sleeve on main axle being provided to ensure sufficient adhesion. The winding shaft runs in two metal or wood bearings, and has the end of a strong thread secured to it for a rope. The other details for the working of this part of the apparatus are perhaps shown clearly enough in the drawings.

If carefully and neatly made, it is wonderful how interesting such a model will prove. In a stiff breeze the sails will revolve at a great rate, and the crane will lift say half a pound at a good speed. Weights will of course be in the form of small sacks of material, boxes, barrels, etc., and the crane should be made capable of slewing so that the loads can be deposited where required. Even in the light winds it is of interest to see the sails moving gently round, and indeed at such a time the appearance is rather more realistic, which may partly compensate for the lessened utility.

CHAPTER III

A SMALL AMERICAN TYPE WINDMILL

The design given in this chapter is intended to form a link between the model pure and simple and the "small power" mill able to perform solid work. It has been thought desirable to admit a certain amount of pattern-making and machining in this case, as a windmill of this size ought to be made on "practical" lines, although it is as simple as possible in construction, and quite within the range of the amateur with a small back-geared lathe. The outside diameter of the sails is 3 feet.

As in all the other cases, the present design may be modified here and there to suit individual fancies, and it may also be reduced to form a very pretty model or enlarged to any reasonable size. Of course, any such change will involve certain alterations in sizes of parts—not necessarily to scale, as, for example, in the case of a mill three times the size, the thicknesses of metal would not in all cases need to be three times as great.

A small machine like this may be recommended particularly for experimental work. The horse-power available in the usual 16-mile breeze

may be estimated at $\frac{1}{30}$ H.P., but this may easily
be doubled in any stiffish wind, so that for many
small matters the power is not to be despised.
With an efficient pump quite a respectable
amount of water can be lifted, or an old boiler
may be pumped up with air pressure, which will
thus be available for running model steam-en-
gines, or for testing purposes, or even a small
blow-lamp, etc. There is no reason why a model
dynamo and accumulator plant should not be
designed to utilise the power. On an average, a
breeze of 16 miles per hour or over is available
for quite six hours a day throughout the year.
Now a mill of the size here described would run
a 6-watt dynamo easily, if of good, efficient construction; so that the normal output for a week's
work would be 6 watts $\times$ 6 hours $\times$ 7 days$=$
252 watt-hours, provided the accumulator were
able to store all it received. Such a result would
be quite attainable during the majority of weeks
in a year.

To get the above result some simple apparatus
in the way of automatic cut-in and cut-out gear
would be required, and the cells would probably
have to be so connected that they could be
charged in parallel and discharged in series.
Thus, the stored energy might be utilised at the
rate of 24 volts, in which case the owner would
be able to get a return of say 2.5 amperes for
four hours (24 V. $\times$ 2.5 amp. $\times$ 4 hours $=$ 240
watt-hours). Undoubtedly there are many cases

where such a result would be regarded as of great utility in the amateur's workshop. Some attention will be paid in the later pages of this

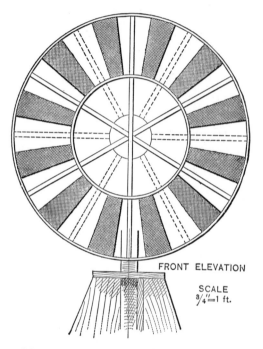

FRONT ELEVATION

SCALE
$\frac{3}{4}''=1$ ft.

Fig. 23.—Model "American" Windmill: Front View of Wheel.

book to the detailed apparatus necessary to this end.

The American type of mill has been adopted in the present instance as much for variety as for other reasons. It is not noticeably more

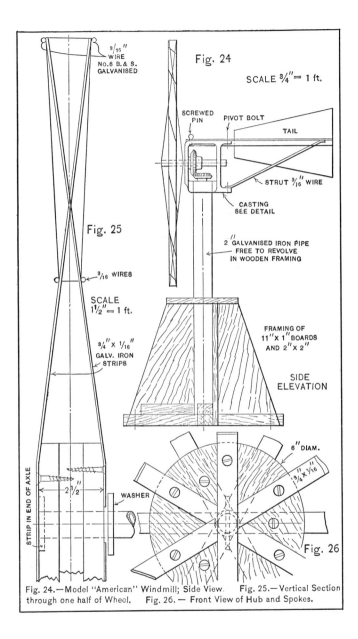

Fig. 24

SCALE ³/₄" = 1 ft.

³/₁₅" WIRE No.6 B.& S. GALVANISED

SCREWED PIN

PIVOT BOLT

TAIL

STRUT ³/₁₆" WIRE

CASTING SEE DETAIL

2" GALVANISED IRON PIPE FREE TO REVOLVE IN WOODEN FRAMING

Fig. 25

³/₁₆ WIRES

SCALE 1¹/₂" = 1 ft.

³/₄" X ¹/₁₆" GALV. IRON STRIPS

FRAMING OF 11"x 1" BOARDS AND 2" X 2"

SIDE ELEVATION

STRIP IN END OF AXLE

2¹/₂"

WASHER

6" DIAM.

³/₄" X ¹/₁₆"

Fig. 26

Fig. 24.—Model "American" Windmill; Side View.   Fig. 25.—Vertical Section through one half of Wheel.   Fig. 26. — Front View of Hub and Spokes.

efficient than some other forms, but lends itself
to simplicity of construction. No attempt has
been made to have the sails self-regulating, but
a tail has been adopted in order to keep the mill
automatically head to wind, and this makes it

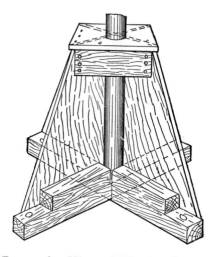

FIG. 27.—Perspective View of Wooden Support for Model
"American" Mill.

easy to regulate the speed by hand or to throw
the mill out of work entirely when desired. This
refinement can, however, be dispensed with if
desired. The size of the wheel is 3 feet in diameter, and its normal speed in a 16-mile breeze
should be from 200 to 250 revolutions per minute.
Front and side views of the complete mill are
shown in figs. 23 and 24 respectively. The whole

of the mill has been designed in metal, as it is intended for constant outdoor work in all weathers.

Commencing with the " tower," this has been reduced to the simplest form by making use of

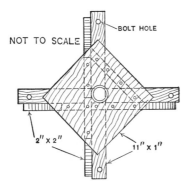

Fig. 28.—Plan of the above.

a piece of old 2-inch gas-, water-, or steam-pipe about 3 feet long. It is desirable that this should have been galvanised, and it must of course be quite straight. The tube is carried in a strong wooden framework of 11 × 1 boards and some 2 × 2 scantlings, so that it can revolve therein without shake or " give," since it will form the movable part of the mill and will carry the whole of the gearing. This wooden framing appears in fig. 24, and is further illustrated in perspective and in plan in figs. 27 and 28 respectively.

The construction of the wheel is indicated in

the vertical section through it in fig. 25 (which is twice the scale of the general arrangement, fig. 24), and also in the perspective drawing, fig.

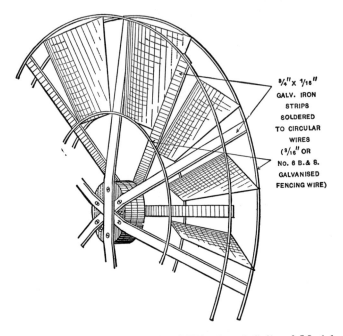

¾" x ¹⁄₁₆"
GALV. IRON
STRIPS
SOLDERED
TO CIRCULAR
WIRES
(³⁄₁₆" OR
NO. 6 B.& S.
GALVANISED
FENCING WIRE)

Fig. 29.—Perspective Sketch of Wheel and Sails of Model "American" Windmill.

29. A hub, formed from three pieces of board, and turned 6 inches diameter, is secured to the shaft by means of an iron strip laid in the saw-cuts in end of shaft, as shown in fig. 30. Nails or screws make the three pieces of wood practically one solid whole.

Referring to fig. 29, it will be seen that the

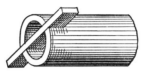

FIG. 30.—Method of Securing Hub on End of Shaft.

wheel is carried by arms or spokes of $\frac{3}{4}$-inch $\times$ $\frac{1}{16}$-inch galvanised hoop-iron.   Six of these spokes start from each side of hub, those on the

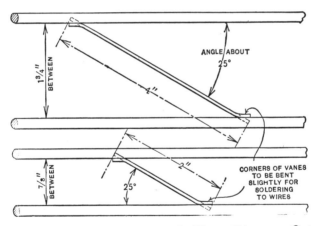

FIG. 31.—Wire Rings for Wheel: Upper Diagram, Outer Rings; Lower Diagram, Inner Rings.

front side being made of three full-length strips, as seen in figs. 23 and 26.   Turning to fig. 25, it will be seen how these spokes cross from front

to back, and *vice versa*. They are also soldered
to four rings, clearly shown in fig. 29, wherever
they cross these latter, and these rings are so
designed as to carry the sails between them.
The rings are of No. 6 B. & S. galvanised fencing wire, carefully curved to accurate diameters
—the outer 36 inches, and the inner 18 inches—
and ends overlapped 2 or 3 inches, bound with
fine wire and soldered together. The proper
distances apart of the two sets of rings are $1\frac{3}{4}$
inches and $\frac{7}{8}$ inch respectively, as shown in fig.
31, which shows also the angle at which the sails
will lie between them, namely about 25°. The
shape of the sails themselves is shown in fig.
32: they should be of thin sheet-zinc, the four
corners slightly bent to lie flat against the wire
rings to give rather more surface for soldering.

If the mill is to be used for " power " production in the ordinary way, it is very difficult to
find a better means of transmitting the energy
than by the usual method of bevel-wheels, as
shown in fig. 24. The exact ratio of one wheel
to the other is only determined by the requirements of the case, and as shown in the drawings
the vertical shaft would make three revolutions
to two of the axle. The wind-wheel and its axle
are carried in a light iron-casting, given in detail in fig. 33, the lower end of which is bored
out to fit tight on the main 2-inch upright tube.
The manner of this fitting, and the arrangement
of bevel-wheels and brass bearings for upper and

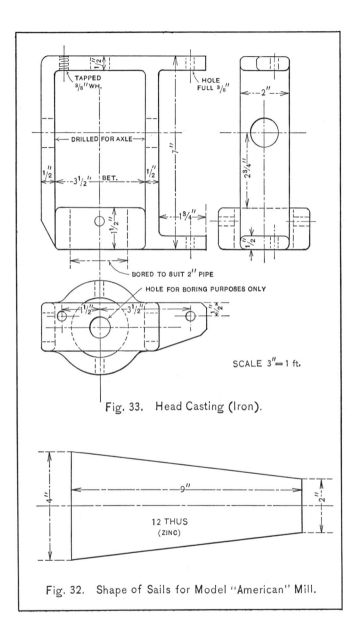

TAPPED
⅜"WH.

HOLE
FULL ⅜"

DRILLED FOR AXLE

7"

½"

½"

3½" BET.

1½"

1¾"

2"

2¾"

½"

BORED TO SUIT 2" PIPE

HOLE FOR BORING PURPOSES ONLY

1½"

3½"

½"

SCALE 3"= 1 ft.

Fig. 33. Head Casting (Iron).

4"

9"

2"

12 THUS
(ZINC)

Fig. 32. Shape of Sails for Model "American" Mill.

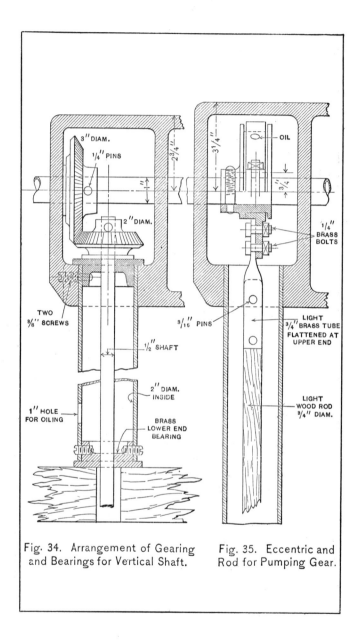

Fig. 34. Arrangement of Gearing
and Bearings for Vertical Shaft.

Fig. 35. Eccentric and
Rod for Pumping Gear.

lower ends of vertical spindle, are shown in fig. 34. There is nothing special in any of these parts, which are all simple turned work.

The machine may be also used to pump water,

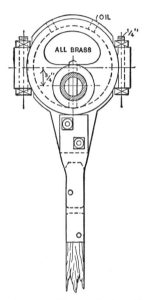

FIG. 36.—Side View of Eccentric for Pumping Gear.

in which case probably the simplest plan is to fit a small eccentric on wind-axle working a connecting-rod with a small pump in lower end of 2-inch tube. To save the reader trouble in designing, a simple eccentric, strap, and rod are shown in figs. 35 and 36, giving a lift of 1½ inches, which of course can be varied to suit the needs of the maker. Too great a lift must be avoided, owing to the speed at which the pump will work. Care must be taken to make the casting (fig. 33) higher than shown, if necessary to enable the eccentric to clear (see fig. 35).

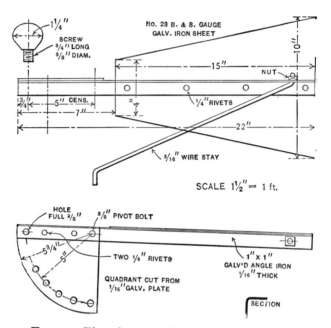

FIG. 37.—Elevation and Plan of Tail Regulator.

Details are given in the drawings, and are probably clearer than written explanations.

The tail-gear, by which the mill is made to face the wind, is detailed in fig. 37, where the upper view is a side elevation and the lower a plan. The tail, formed of thin galvanised sheet-iron, is riveted to a piece of very light galvanised angle of the section shown. This is not the usual *rolled* angle, but bent sheet, much lighter and more suitable for this work. It can be obtained from tank-makers or workers in galvanised sheet-iron. The tail is pivoted where shown by a bolt which allows sufficient movement and is locked in position by the screw shown, a tapped hole being provided in the casting (fig. 33). To get the full effect of wind, the tail must lie square with the wheel, or in line with axle. Should the wind be too high, its effect on the wheel can be diminished by letting the tail turn to an angle of 45° or less with the wheel, inserting the screw in one of the radial holes in quadrant, according to the strength of the breeze. The last hole (at right angles to tail) is the " off " position, as when the screw is in that place the tail will lie parallel with wheel and the effect of wind on same will be nil. The wire stay shown in the drawings supporting back end of tail may be found unnecessary, but is easily fixed.

It will be very desirable to fit a brake to the mill. This need be only a very simple affair—a wooden pulley fitted at any convenient position on the driven shaft, with a rod or lever to press on rim either by weights or spring when desired. This may often be useful when it is required to stop the mill or to alter the setting of tail, or even in the workshop to regulate speed when experimenting.

All parts of the mill subject to the weather should either be galvanised or very well painted if of iron, and a cap of galvanised sheet fitted over the bevel-wheels and casting will not only avoid unsightly rusting, but will save oil and reduce friction.

CHAPTER IV

A Small Working Windmill

The windmill next to claim attention is one that should appeal to a large circle of readers. It has purposely been designed in a very simple form, yet of a size sufficient to develop reasonable power, namely, $\frac{1}{10}$ horse-power in a moderately stiff breeze of say 16 miles an hour. Such a mill will do real work, such as pumping water, running a small grindstone, or even driving a 30-watt dynamo. The total diameter of the wheel is 6 feet.

In order to simplify the machine as far as possible, the mill has been designed with fixed head, so that the wind must be in one of two opposite directions to give a maximum effect. It should therefore be set up with the front wheel facing in the direction of the prevailing wind. Where the two principal prevailing winds are, say, S.W. and N.W., the best direction for the axis of the mill would probably be north and south. Local conditions should be studied, and detailed records of the prevailing winds of the locality can generally be obtained without difficulty. A fixed mill like this is also suitable for a town dweller, where long rows of houses confine the wind to definite directions up and down the line of " back gardens."

The vanes (see figs. 38 and 44) can be either fixed or allowed to revolve partially upon the arms. If fixed, the mill will run in opposite directions with opposite winds, and while this need not matter for such operations as pumping, it would not be satisfactory in other work. A simple device has therefore been adopted, so that when the wind blows from what may be called the back of the mill the sails will automatically reverse and so cause the direction of rotation to be always one way. The maker who prefers to have the sails fixed may ignore this arrangement and screw the vanes firmly to the arms, which need only to be tapered off, and not rounded in section. The alternative arms required in this case are sketched in fig. 46 (two views), and of course require less work on their construction.

The mill, as shown in figs. 38 to 47, has six whips or arms mounted upon a triangular hub to which they are all bolted. The six whips are formed from three hardwood sticks, each making a pair of arms. The sticks will be $1\frac{1}{2}$ inches square in section, 6 feet long, the central portion for a length of 22 inches left square while the ends should be turned down taper, from $1\frac{1}{4}$ inches diameter at the root to 1 inch diameter at the tips. Good, sound, straight wood should be selected.

The hub, shown in detail in fig. 39, should be very carefully made, to an equilateral triangle to the sizes given, of a piece of very sound hardwood of some non-splitting timber. Beech would be suitable. The hole for axle must be truly bored and fit well so that the sails will all run in true plane and square to the axle. The three sticks must be bolted to hub, each with two ⅜-inch galvanised bolts, with good-sized washers, every care being taken to fix each stick at right angles to shaft. For further security, another ¼-inch or ⅜-inch bolt will join each pair of sticks at their crossing, it being noticed that in one case (see fig. 43) a piece of packing of same thickness as the sticks will be required. The bolt in this case must also be so much longer.

The axle, or windshaft, as it was called in older days, will consist in this case of a short length of stout mild steel tubing. The size is not important—it is shown 1 inch diameter outside, and should not be less. This is not so much for strength as for better attachment to the hub with its far-spreading sails. A piece of ¾-inch gas tubing will make a satisfactory axle if centred in lathe and a light skimming taken off to obtain roundness and to make good, clean journals.

The hardwood hub should be fixed to axle by a couple of ¼-inch split pins going right through, as seen in fig. 39. These can easily be got in parallel with two of the sticks, and should fit well so as to allow no backlash.

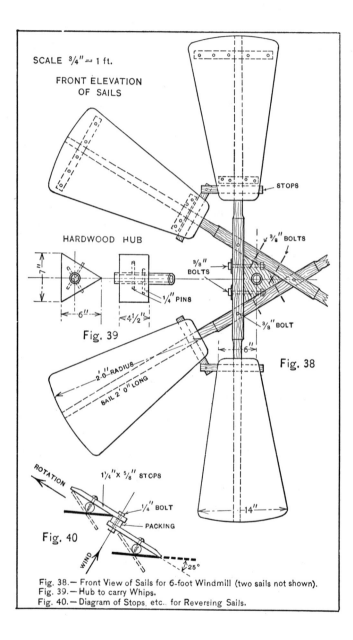

SCALE ¾" = 1 ft.

FRONT ELEVATION
OF SAILS

HARDWOOD HUB

7"

6"

4½"

¼" PINS

Fig. 39

STOPS

⅜" BOLTS

⅜" BOLTS

⅜" BOLT

6"

Fig. 38

2' 0" RADIUS

SAIL 2' 0" LONG

14"

ROTATION

1¼" × ⅝" STOPS

¼" BOLT

PACKING

Fig. 40

WIND

25°

Fig. 38.— Front View of Sails for 6-foot Windmill (two sails not shown).
Fig. 39.— Hub to carry Whips.
Fig. 40.— Diagram of Stops, etc., for Reversing Sails.

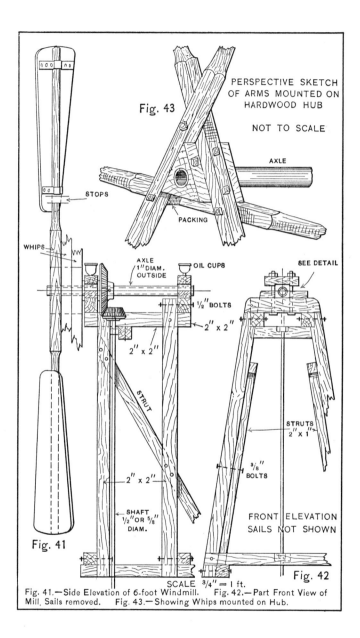

Fig. 43

PERSPECTIVE SKETCH
OF ARMS MOUNTED ON
HARDWOOD HUB

NOT TO SCALE

AXLE

STOPS

PACKING

WHIPS

AXLE
1" DIAM.
OUTSIDE

OIL CUPS

SEE DETAIL

1/2" BOLTS

2" x 2"

2" x 2"

STRUT

2" x 2"

STRUTS
2" x 1"

3/8"
BOLTS

SHAFT
1/2" OR 5/8"
DIAM.

FRONT ELEVATION
SAILS NOT SHOWN

Fig. 41

Fig. 42

SCALE 3/4" = 1 ft.

Fig. 41.—Side Elevation of 6-foot Windmill.   Fig. 42.—Part Front View of
Mill, Sails removed.   Fig. 43.—Showing Whips mounted on Hub.

The bearings should certainly be of brass, and the most simple form they can very well take is that shown in fig. 47. This provides, of course, no adjustment— a refinement that can be adopted with advantage if desired, but which hardly needs illustration. These bearings are carried in hardwood " pedestals," and secured by hardwood caps bolted down over them. A recess is made in cap and blocks are provided on base to prevent side movement of brasses. If possible, oil cups or other similar lubricators should be fitted, but they *may* be dispensed with if the oil can is kept going. A cover of thin sheet-iron, galvanised, may be fitted with advantage to the working parts. The details of forward bearing are sufficiently indicated in the three views, fig. 47; the back end bearing being exactly the same. Every care should be taken to make all tight and avoid any rocking.

The power of the mill may best be transmitted by means of a pair of bevel-wheels, as shown in fig. 41. This is the usual method, and of course various ratios of speed can be got according to the wheels used. As here shown, the wheels have a speed ratio of two to one; and a light, true-running shaft, say $\frac{5}{8}$ inch or even $\frac{1}{2}$ inch diameter, carries the lower wheel. If this shaft must be of any great length, or if much of it must be unsupported, a greater diameter is desirable; here again tubing can be substituted for solid rod. For pumping purposes a crank may

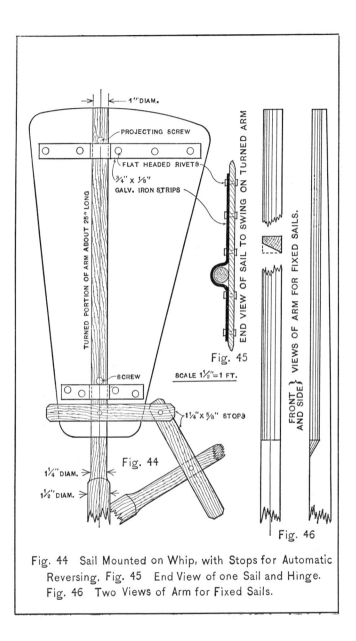

Fig. 44 Sail Mounted on Whip, with Stops for Automatic
Reversing. Fig. 45 End View of one Sail and Hinge.
Fig. 46 Two Views of Arm for Fixed Sails.

be arranged either as an overhung crank on tail
end of shaft, by an eccentric as described in the
last chapter, or by cranking the shaft itself, the
throw being made suitable for the pump to be
used. A light wooden connecting-rod should be
used if this plan is adopted.

The method of carrying the vanes and also
the device for automatically swinging them to
suit the wind are shown in figs. 40, 44, and 45.
The vanes are each formed of one (or, if necessary, of two) ⅜-inch boards, the edges being
tapered off as shown in fig. 45. Any timber not
liable to warp in sun and weather will be suitable, one of the best being Californian redwood,
usually obtainable in wide sizes.

The supports or hinges, clearly seen in fig. 44,
are of ¾-inch × ⅛-inch galvanised hoop-iron
neatly bent to fit round the arms at the places
assigned to them. They are attached to the
vanes by ¼-inch flat-headed rivets or bolts, galvanised by preference, with large washers next
the wood, as shown. A good screw projecting
from the arm just beyond each bearing prevents
the vane from slipping off. It should be seen
that each vane swings easily but without shake.

Owing to the unbalanced shape of the sails,
they will swing according to the direction of
the wind, and means are provided to allow them
to take up a position either way at the best angle
for general work. This is specially shown in fig.
40, in which the black lines show how the sails

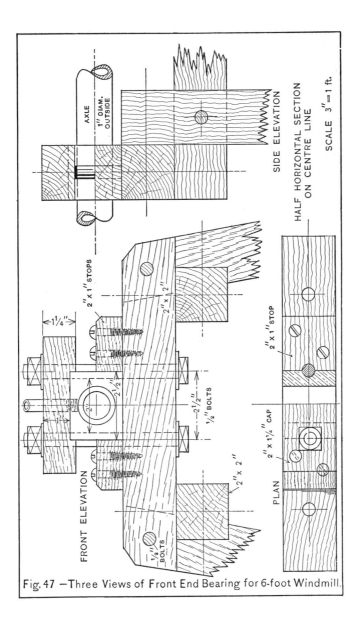

Fig. 47 —Three Views of Front End Bearing for 6-foot Windmill.

would set with the wind in the direction given, and the direction of rotation for same. The dotted lines indicate the condition when the wind blows from the opposite quarter. The device consists of pairs of short cross-bars screwed to backs of arms and bolted, with packing between, at their crossing. As the angle each way is important, care must be taken, by cutting away the cross-bars or providing packing, if either is necessary, to secure an angle of about 25°. A template cut to the correct angle should be used to adjust the vanes in each case.

The timber framing on which the mill is erected needs no description beyond that afforded by the sketches, but it should be remembered that stiffness is essential not only for safety but also to avoid strain on the vertical shaft and loss of power. Cross-bars can be bolted in at intervals if this shaft is long, and bearings fitted upon them.

A final word is necessary as to painting. For such an "outside job" as a windmill careful painting is essential, and in particular each piece of finished timber in the mill itself must be very carefully painted over before being built up. Three coats of the best paint will not be too much, and the last coat may be advantageously mixed with some thoroughly good "outside" varnish. The next season after erection, another two coats of paint should be applied, but probably longer intervals may then elapse between the applications. Attention should always be paid to regular oiling, and it will be wise to avoid working the mill unnecessarily by fitting a brake or locking mechanism in some convenient position indoors. Indeed, a brake may be very desirable as a means of preventing accident either to work or person if the windmill is used for driving a lathe or other machine.

CHAPTER V

A Practical Working Windmill

To complete the series of small windmills suitable for amateur workmanship, a really practical machine, capable of "power" production on a moderate scale, remains to be described. It is thought that a mill of 10-feet diameter, while probably taxing to the fullest the constructive ability of any average reader, might well be attempted by a serious worker with happy results. In this instance, while preserving the general principle of simplicity, completeness has been aimed at, and castings and forgings are adopted throughout without hesitation. This certainly involves some pattern-making, which, however, should be within the scope of any one able to carry out the necessary machining of the castings. Some readers may be willing—and able— to reduce this part of the labour by adopting makeshift details, but it should be remembered that such a method is hardly more advisable than it would be in the case of building any other motor—say a steam-engine—for power production.

The rating for a 10-foot windmill would be about ¼ H.P., which probably appears small for

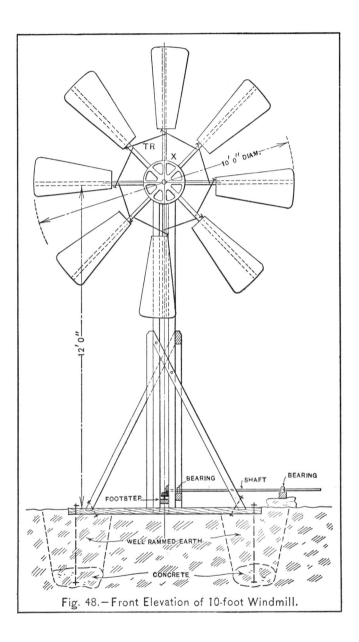

TR

X

10' 0" DIAM.

12' 0"

BEARING   SHAFT   BEARING

FOOTSTEP

WELL RAMMED EARTH

CONCRETE

Fig. 48.—Front Elevation of 10-foot Windmill.

the amount of work involved and the material employed. It is, however, a conservative estimate, and is based on the standard 16-mile breeze, which holds good for something like 8 hours per day on two-thirds of the days in the year. Manufacturers probably rate a mill of this size much higher, and as long as no wind-velocity is stated, they may fairly claim to be correct. All practical modern windmills, however, are constructed with automatic gear so that with any given velocity of wind a maximum output is obtained, and any increase in the wind is more or less counteracted by the action of the automatic gear. It follows therefore that if our 10-foot mill is set to produce say $\frac{1}{2}$ H.P., it can only do this with a wind of much higher velocity than 16 miles per hour, which is also much more rare. Nevertheless, it will be quite within the maker's power to get as much as this and more out of his machine, if he so desires and the wind is there. It will be merely a question of altering the controlling weight, but will also involve very much heavier stresses on the machine. This point must be borne in mind.

A general elevation is given in fig. 48, to a scale of $\frac{1}{4}$ inch to the foot. The tower is built up of four 3 inches $\times$ 3 inches vertical members, 12 feet high, each placed at the corners of a square, with 4-inch space between each pair of uprights. These uprights are well braced by struts, also of 3 $\times$ 3 timber, starting below the circle of

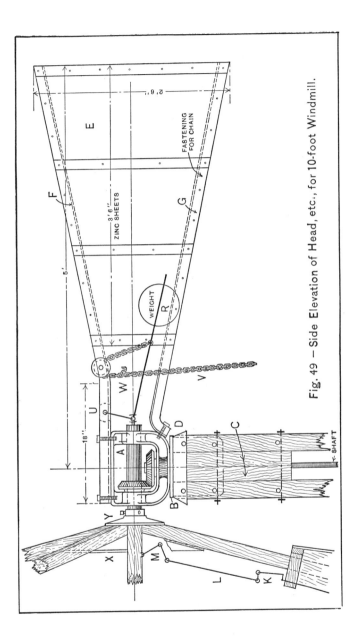

Fig. 49 — Side Elevation of Head, etc., for 10-foot Windmill.

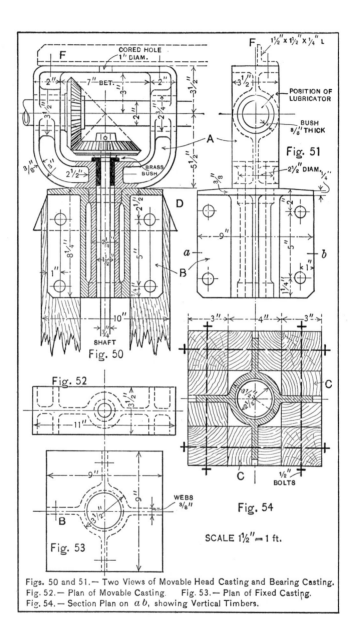

CORED HOLE 1" DIAM.

F

2" 7" BET. 2"

3"

2"

3½"

3½"

5½"

A

3" BRASS BUSH

2½"

D

2½"

8¼"

2¼"

1½"

1"

5"

¾"

B

10"

¾"

SHAFT

Fig. 50

F 1½" x 1½" x ¼" L

3½"

POSITION OF LUBRICATOR

BUSH ⅜" THICK

Fig. 51

2½" DIAM ¼"

⅜

9"

a

2"

5"

b

1"

1¼"

Fig. 52

3½"

11"

3" 4" 3"

C

⅜"

½"

C

½" BOLTS

WEBS ⅜"

Fig. 54

B

9"

3½"

9"

Fig. 53

SCALE 1½" = 1 ft.

Figs. 50 and 51.— Two Views of Movable Head Casting and Bearing Casting.
Fig. 52.— Plan of Movable Casting.   Fig. 53.— Plan of Fixed Casting.
Fig. 54.— Section Plan on $a\,b$, showing Vertical Timbers.

vanes, one strut on each side, and each bolted
to two uprights, as shown. The lower ends of
struts are lodged into two horizontal diagonals,
which are halved over each other at their crossing so as to lie level. The lower ends of uprights
with a little shaping will also fit alongside these
diagonals and must be securely bolted to them
with ½-inch bolts. Bolts or straps must also secure the diagonals to the feet of struts. Four
¾-inch bolts not less than 3 feet long must be
carried down at the four ends of the horizontal
members, into pockets of rough concrete of 2 or
3 cubic feet each. The holes above the concrete
must be then very firmly filled in and rammed,
and if the ground is soft or yielding, a greater
depth and more concrete must be employed. It
is perhaps needless to insist on the importance
of having all this timber, but especially that in
contact with the ground, thoroughly well tarred,
or better still, properly creosoted, and all bolts
should be galvanised. Large thick washers
under the nuts of the ¾-inch bolts are required.

A more detailed side elevation of the head,
tail, and part of the arms is given in fig. 49, to
a scale of ¾ inch to the foot. This shows the
movable head casting A carried on the bearing
casting B. Both these are detailed still further,
to a scale of 1½ inches to the foot in figs. 50 to
54, and require little explanation. The stem of
A is of course turned to ride easily in the bored
hole in B, and is fitted with brass bushes for

axle and for vertical shaft. The casting B is securely bolted to the tops of the 3 × 3 uprights with ½-inch bolts, care being taken to get it truly upright and central with the timbers. Packing pieces, C, in figs. 49 and 54, are used to ensure correct spacing. Note should be taken of the sheet of zinc or lead, D, figs. 49 and 50, which is first laid on tops of uprights, with suitable hole in middle to allow stem of B to pass, and is then dressed down, as shown, to throw all water from the timbers. It should hang clear of the latter to avoid capillary action.

The tail, employed to keep the mill up to the wind, is also shown in fig. 49 at E. It is carried by two light angles, 1½ inches × 1½ inches × ¼ inch, F and G, which are bolted respectively to the top and bottom of head casting A with ⅜-inch bolts. The position of these angles is indicated (in dotted lines) in figs. 50 and 51 at F. A sheet of zinc forms the tail surface and is riveted to angles with ¼-inch rivets about 4½ inches' pitch. Four stiffeners of 1¼ inch × ⅛-inch hoop-iron run vertically across the surface, dividing it into three equal spaces. Both angles and stiffening strips should be galvanised.

The shaping of one of the eight arms for the vanes is shown in fig. 55, and the outline of sail in fig. 56. The assembling of these parts is indicated in fig. 49, but it is necessary to turn to fig. 57 to see in greater detail not only the method of fixing but also the formidable-looking array of levers and rods constituting the automatic gear. Every one of the eight sails has its independent set of levers to actuate the central

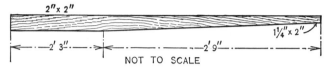

FIG. 55.—Shaping of Arm or Whip.

sliding rod, but while it must be admitted this means a rather long list of troublesome details, the complication is much more apparent than real, and is largely due to the difficulty of ren-

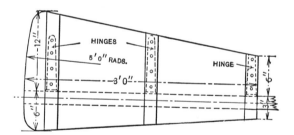

FIG. 56.—Outline of Sail for 10-foot Windmill.

dering in a drawing the working of levers that do not lie in the same plane. The reader is therefore asked to study with some care these drawings, which the author for his part believes to be presented as simply as possible. All that has really to be remembered is that the wind impinging on an unbalanced sail attempts to turn it on its hinges, as shown in plan in fig. 58. Regarding now the short side of sail (the so-called " leading sail "), it of course describes an arc of rather less than a right angle, until it lies flat in the plane of the wind's direction. The chord of this arc, or rather of that described by a projecting pin J (a piece of $\frac{5}{16}$-inch rod bent as shown), forms the path of the lower arm of lever K, fully drawn in fig. 64, the other arm of which, being at right angles, must move vertically up and down as compared with the sail movement. This actuates the $\frac{3}{8}$-inch rod L (detailed in figs. 59 and 60), which in its turn works lever M. As before indicated, the planes of movement of the levers K and M are not coincident, but while this makes their representation on paper less easy, it in no way affects the object, which is to produce on the sliding rod N an in-and-out movement according to the amount of the wind's pressure. The lever K is supported at the special angle required (seen in plan in fig. 58) by a bracket O (fig. 64) bolted to arm. The top arm of lever is made with a return end in order to give a long bearing, and bottom end slotted to allow the necessary play for the pin J, due to the path of the latter being an arc.

Returning now to the sliding rod N, it will be seen that the motion of the eight levers M is transmitted to it through the special turned nut P, figs. 62 and 63. The various possible positions of the forked end of lever require that the section of this " nut " be turned to the curves shown. A lock-nut on the outer side enables P to be screwed up to the most suitable position, and there secured in place by the lock-nut.

Examination will show that the tendency of any wind action on the sail is to force rod L nearer the centre of mill, and so to drive rod N to the right as looked at in figs. 49 and 57. This has to be met at the other end of N by the counteraction of a weight, R, carried by a cranked lever, S, indicated in a diagram in fig. 49, and more fully in figs. 67 and 69. The lever, the short end of which is doubled or looped (see left-hand view in fig. 67) in order to pass on both sides of the loose pin bearing T, is hung from the upper tail-angle F by a $\frac{1}{2}$-inch screw, a securer bearing being obtained for this by tapping into the block U, which is riveted to angle, see section, fig. 68. The arrangement of end of rod N and pin block T is more clearly shown in fig. 69. Fig. 65 gives an end view of pin bearing, T.

The weight, R, should be cast double, one piece having a slot or recess cast on one side as shown in fig. 66. It is difficult to fix on the exact weight that may be required, as this depends not only on the views of the maker as to the power which he desires the mill to exert at its maximum, but also on the friction of the numerous joints in levers. It is, however, recommended that a trial be made with a weight of

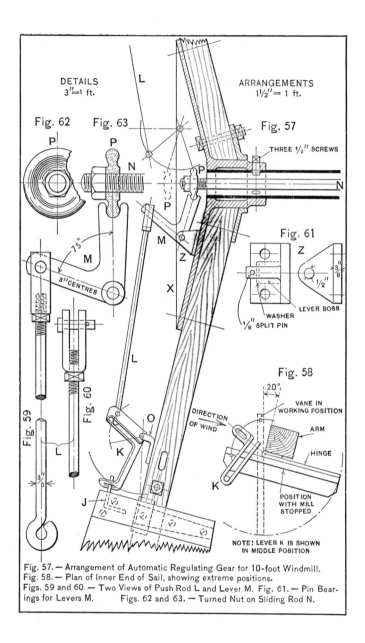

DETAILS
3″=1 ft.

ARRANGEMENTS
1½″= 1 ft.

Fig. 62   Fig. 63   L   Fig. 57

P   P   N

THREE ½″ SCREWS

N

P

P

M   M   Z   Fig. 61

Z

75°   X

3″CENTRES   ¾″⅜

½″

LEVER BOSS

WASHER
⅛″ SPLIT PIN

Fig. 60   L   Fig. 58

20°

VANE IN
WORKING POSITION

O   DIRECTION
OF WIND   ARM

Fig. 59   K   HINGE

L   K

¾″   J   POSITION
WITH MILL
STOPPED

NOTE: LEVER K IS SHOWN
IN MIDDLE POSITION

Fig. 57.—Arrangement of Automatic Regulating Gear for 10-foot Windmill.
Fig. 58.—Plan of Inner End of Sail, showing extreme positions.
Figs. 59 and 60.—Two Views of Push Rod L and Lever M. Fig. 61.—Pin Bearings for Levers M.   Figs. 62 and 63.—Turned Nut on Sliding Rod N.

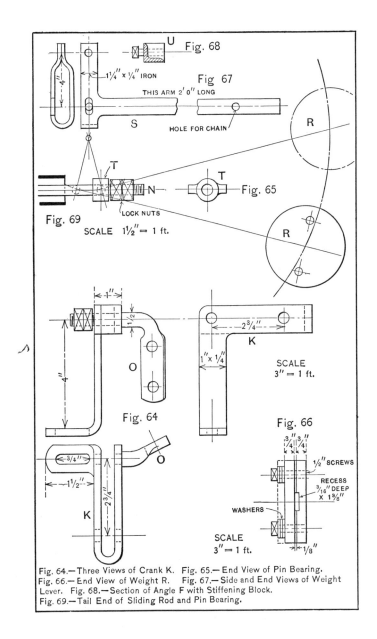

U Fig. 68

$1\frac{1}{4}'' \times \frac{1}{4}''$ IRON

Fig 67

THIS ARM 2' 0" LONG

4"

S

HOLE FOR CHAIN

R

T

T

N

Fig. 65

LOCK NUTS

Fig. 69

SCALE $1\frac{1}{2}'' = 1$ ft.

R

1"

$\frac{1}{2}$

O

4"

Fig. 64

K

$2\frac{3}{4}''$

$1'' \times \frac{1}{4}$

SCALE
$3'' = 1$ ft.

Fig. 66

$\frac{3}{4}''$ $\frac{3}{4}''$

$\frac{1}{2}''$ SCREWS

RECESS
$\frac{3}{16}''$ DEEP
$\times 1\frac{3}{8}''$

WASHERS

$\frac{3}{4}''$

$1\frac{1}{2}''$

$2\frac{3}{4}$

O

K

SCALE
$3'' = 1$ ft.

$\frac{1}{8}''$

Fig. 64.—Three Views of Crank K. Fig. 65.— End View of Pin Bearing.
Fig. 66.— End View of Weight R.   Fig. 67.— Side and End Views of Weight
Lever. Fig. 68.— Section of Angle F with Stiffening Block.
Fig. 69.— Tail End of Sliding Rod and Pin Bearing.

about 10 lbs., corresponding with the full lines
in the drawings given. If the mill sails are
found to open too easily with this weight—which
is, however, doubtful—it can be shifted further
along the lever arm, or if even this is found
insufficient, another disc can be added as shown
dotted on the left in fig. 66. A light galvanised
chain, running over a pulley in top angle of
tail and hanging with a loop to within 6 feet of
the ground level, is used to lift weight when the
owner desires to stop the mill, this action, of
course, opening all the sails so as to present only
their edges to the wind. The other end of chain
is looped back to a point near outer end of tail
to avoid entanglement with uprights or running
shaft. A hook attached to chain in proper position, W, can be hitched under lower angle of
tail by taking chain sideways a little and so hang
the weight up for any length of time.

The automatic action and its details should
now be fairly clear, and the remaining parts of
the mill are simple. The large central casting,
X, appears in several figures, notably in section
in fig. 57 and in front elevation in fig. 70. It is
undoubtedly the most serious undertaking in the
whole construction and must probably be " put
out " into the hands of professionals. It should
not, however, be a costly item, and if made as
indicated will go far to making the mill a practical job. This casting carries the eight arms
and makes secure connection to the axle. It is

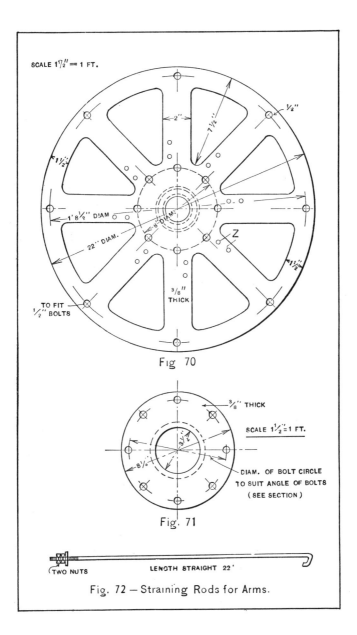

SCALE 1½" = 1 FT.

2"

7½"

½"

1½"

1'8½" DIAM

8" DIAM

22" DIAM.

Z

³/₈" THICK

TO FIT ½" BOLTS

Fig 70

³/₈" THICK

SCALE 1½"= 1 FT.

3½"

8½"

DIAM. OF BOLT CIRCLE TO SUIT ANGLE OF BOLTS (SEE SECTION)

Fig. 71

TWO NUTS

LENGTH STRAIGHT 22'

Fig. 72 — Straining Rods for Arms.

backed up in its support of the arms by the
smaller annular casting Y, fig. 71, which is bored
to fit well over turned part of X. Three very
well-fitted $\frac{1}{2}$-inch screws at 120° secure the boss
to shaft, a good tight fit between shaft and casting
being essential. These screws must not project
inside the shaft far enough to touch the sliding
rod N.

The casting X carries also the eight little
brackets Z for the levers M. These brackets are
of cast iron and may be "American" in character in so far that the pins form part of the
casting, a file probably being a good enough tool
to finish them.

A little further stiffening of the sail-arms is
obtained by the use of the tension-rods TR, detailed in fig. 72. These are only $\frac{1}{4}$-inch galvanised rods one end turned over for an inch at
right angles and the other screwed and lock-
nutted. The tension put on these must be even
and not too great; but they, as well as other
screws and bolts in the machine, will probably
require tightening up once or twice when the
weather has had its effect on the timber.

A word is required in reference to this latter
item. The arms should certainly be wrought
from good sound seasoned ash. The sails can
hardly be formed of better timber than Californian redwood (*Sequoia semper virens*), which
can be obtained in wide boards. They will be
$\frac{1}{2}$ inch thick with the edges chamfered off both

sides. Three battens, 2 inches $\times$ 1¼ of sound hardwood (ash, bluegum, etc.) must be well screwed across, and the hinges, three in number, will come opposite these, on the other side of sail. These hinges should be of the strongest make of T shape, galvanised. They are shown in the plan, fig. 58.

So far the axle has hardly been mentioned. It is, however, a very simple matter, being nothing but a piece of 2-inch (outside diameter) steel steam-pipe, preferably solid drawn, and quite ¼ inch thick. It should be true to begin with, so that the very lightest skimming in the lathe will make it a good journal. It carries the usual bevel-wheel, indicated in figs. 49 and 57, and gearing with another of the same size on the vertical shaft. Both wheels are 4 inches on inner diameters, but may be more or less if required, the casting A being altered if necessary. The vertical spindle would be a piece of ¾-inch cold rolled steel shafting, and should have bearings also at bottom end and half-way down the tower, presuming the spindle is carried down to the ground as shown in fig. 48. A pair of bevel-wheels is also required to transmit power to a horizontal shaft.

One or two points in conclusion deserve remark. First, that all possible metal parts should be either galvanised or of sheet zinc. The castings will most probably be only painted. They should be "pickled," freed from rust and especially from dirt and grease, and painted with good red lead paint well rubbed in. It is better still to warm the castings to about 100° Fahr. when putting the first coat on. Three coats of the red lead paint, thinly put on, and a finishing coat of grey or black paint are required to make a good job. The woodwork, it has already been remarked, should be tarred or creosoted. This does not apply to the arms and vanes, all of which require the usual painting in most thorough fashion. The most suitable paint is pure white lead with a dash of ochre.

Steps, formed from any suitable timber, say 3 × 2 inches, should be nailed up at least two sides of the verticals to enable the owner to reach the head of mill for oiling, etc.

A mill of this power, especially if used to drive a lathe or other workshop tools, should have a simple cut-out device—such as a sliding coupling actuated by a handy cord or chain, so as to throw the mill out of gear in case of an accident. A brake is not so necessary, as the automatic gear is designed as much as possible to keep the machine at uniform speed. Under normal output this speed should be from 80 to 100 revs. per minute, varying slightly according to the setting of the sails. These, in their flattest position—that is, with a light wind—should lie at an angle of about 20° to the plane of revolution of the wheel.

CHAPTER VI

Production of Electricity by Wind-Power

To most readers the possibility of applying the power from a windmill to the production of electrical energy will be an interesting feature, and it is fortunate that recent experimental work has proved that not only is this feasible but even simple, inexpensive, and reliable. By "reliability" it is not, of course, meant that the fickleness of the wind is completely overcome, but only that the apparatus, which includes some automatic gear, can be relied upon not to go wrong. It is certainly possible—within reasonable limits—by employing a large enough mill and accumulator, to tide over even extensive calms, but probably any amateur engineer who decides to adopt the method to be described will be willing to accept a few inevitable "off-days" in each year, when no current will be available, balancing this trouble against the very definite advantage of the inexpensiveness of the power.

Many experiments have been made at different times and in different places to utilise wind-power in the way now under discussion. There is, however, no need to deal with more than one, which, having proved satisfactory in practice, is in use in a fairly large number of instances in North Germany and in Denmark, not only for the supply of isolated farm-houses but even for village lighting and power production. In practically all these cases an oil-engine is used as a standby, yet it is found that the number of days in the year on which this engine is called into use are so few that the reader who proposes to light a house or provide himself with power on a small scale may reasonably consider the extra expense unnecessary in his case.

The following suggestions are based entirely on the excellent work recently done and published by Prof. P. la Cour in Denmark on behalf of that Government, which has in that particular placed itself ahead of other countries—considerably to the advantage of many of its villages and isolated dwellings. The reader must be prepared to experiment a little—not indeed in principles but in details of apparatus to suit his own case—but may rest absolutely assured that the method is quite practical and satisfactory.

There are two main difficulties in applying a power so variable and intermittent as wind to the production and supply of electricity. There must, first, be a means of automatically switching on the dynamo to a set of accumulators whenever the former is in a position to deliver current, the same apparatus cutting it out when the power falls away. Secondly, means must be adopted whereby an increase of wind-power beyond the normal amount required to just work the dynamo shall not affect the output by increasing either voltage or current. Both these ends have been attained by La Cour with the simplest apparatus imaginable.

A consideration of the second question raised will show why it is necessary to decide on a definite wind-velocity as being that at which any given windmill shall supply its "normal" output. By rating it low, say a wind of 9 miles per hour, it is possible to keep a dynamo working nearly every day in the year and for twelve hours out of the twenty-four. But the power of the wind at 9 miles an hour is only a quarter of that at 15 miles an hour, and although the latter only blows about half the total number of days in a year, and then for only about nine or ten hours a day, its total output is greater than the other. Another point to be considered is that a very small dynamo is much less efficient, so that a double loss is experienced if too much constancy of work is aimed at. Of course, in a large installation these points have less emphasis, and it becomes desirable to run the plant at a lower wind-rating (in other words, use a comparatively large mill), the only limiting factor being the initial cost of the plant.

In a wind-driven generating plant the following points should be noted. The windmill itself should be self-regulating (as, for example, that described in Chap. V.), and fitted with tail so as to turn to face all possible winds. The dynamo should be shunt-wound, so that an increase in the external resistance tends to raise the terminal voltage. If necessary, this tendency may be increased by having one or two resistance coils in series with the shunt-winding, these coils being automatically cut out as the external resistance rises and current falls. A low-speed machine is certainly preferable, the speed of a windmill being rather low itself. The accumulator is a vital point: it should have a large capacity, as on this depends its ability to maintain a supply over a longer period of calm; yet, as it is undesirable for any accumulator to remain long at a low state of charging, care must be taken to avoid draining it—especially if a spell of calm weather seems likely.

The whole of the electrical apparatus is shown diagrammatically in fig. 73, the only part needing much description being the automatic switch, further illustrated in three views in fig. 74. This consists of two electro-magnets, EM, each like an ordinary bell-magnet, and wound with fine wire, but with an extra winding of a few turns of thick wire, exactly like a compound-wound dynamo field magnet. A horse-shoe permanent magnet, PM, is suspended so that its poles lie opposite and near to the poles of the electro-magnets, and swings by means of the

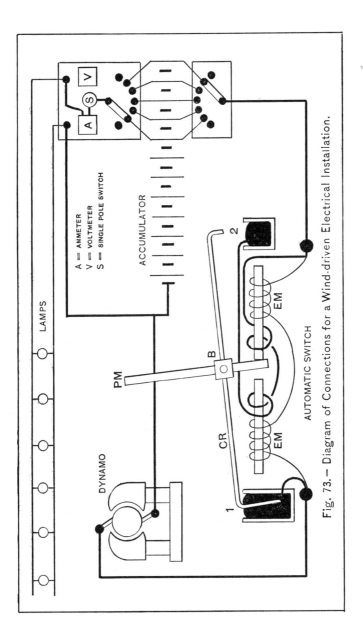

LAMPS

A = AMMETER
V = VOLTMETER
S = SINGLE POLE SWITCH

ACCUMULATOR

DYNAMO

PM

CR

B

EM

EM

1

2

AUTOMATIC SWITCH

Fig. 73. — Diagram of Connections for a Wind-driven Electrical Installation.

pivot screws which work in a *brass* (or non-magnetic) block, B. This block also carries the copper rod CR, each end of which turns downward into the wooden cups 1 and 2, containing mercury, matters being so arranged, however, that the end 1 is always in the mercury whichever way PM is swung, while 2 only touches the mercury when that end of CR is drawn downwards.

The switchboards present no special features. By following out the connections it will be seen that any agreed number of cells can be switched on to the dynamo, while any independent number can be caused to supply the lamps. This latter arrangement is desirable to allow for drop of voltage during discharge, also to provide for losses in mains and for an extra cell or two in case of accident to others.

The action of the automatic switch is as follows: Assuming the dynamo to be still, or running at too low a speed to furnish current, it will be seen that the battery is energising the electro-magnets EM through the fine wire-coils, the current passing also through the armature of the dynamo. The winding of EM is such that the current in this direction attracts the poles of PM to the right and so raises the end, 2, of CR out of the mercury. Only a very small current is required, or allowed, to be thus wasted. Supposing now the wind to increase sufficiently to raise the speed of dynamo so

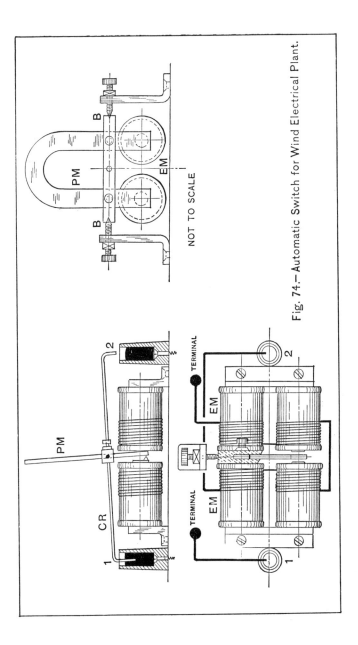

NOT TO SCALE

Fig. 74.—Automatic Switch for Wind Electrical Plant.

much as to be able to supply current, the first
effect will be to reduce the current in EM to
nil and then to reverse it, altering the polarity
of the electro-magnets and throwing the lower
end of magnet PM over to the right. This, by
dipping the end 2 of CR into the mercury,
makes connection between the dynamo and accumulator, the charging of which at once begins.
The effect of the thick-wire coils on EM is to
hold the magnet switch more securely during
charging. The opposite action—that of throwing out the dynamo when the speed fails—is
obvious on inspection.

The apparatus required to maintain the dynamo at the right speed when that of the mill
itself ranges too high is a system of belts and
pulleys, shown in fig. 75. Here A is an ordinary
pulley with the usual curved face; B, a rather
wide, flat-surfaced pulley; C and D, again, ordinary pulleys; C and B being fast on one shaft.
This shaft is carried on the light timber frame
EF, hinged at E, and carrying a weight G at
the other end.

It will be seen that this arrangement provides
for a constant pull on the belt between A and B.
It may be found that this pull is too great even
without the weight G, in which case a cord
(shown dotted) takes its place, and, by means
of a pulley overhead and another weight, takes
off some of the load.

The belt CD has no special feature beyond

being thin, supple, and even. That between A and B, however, must be specially smooth on its running surface, and must in addition be thoroughly well oiled. On this depends the peculiar result to be obtained. It is found that when the weight G has been properly adjusted, and other details of current supply, etc., decided upon by experiment, no matter how much faster than normal A is compelled to run by the wind, the speed of B remains constant or with just sufficient variation to meet the slightly varying conditions required by the dynamo, the belt slipping on B at the higher speeds. The principle, of course, is not new; but its application in the present instance, together with the automatic switch, is an excellent example of mechanical adaptation.

The details of the whole of the apparatus must necessarily be worked out by individual requirements: the following suggestions, however, are added as an example, the instance chosen being the 10-foot windmill described in the last chapter. This windmill, working in a 15- or 16-mile breeze, should have an output of about $\frac{1}{4}$ H.P. Allowing for losses in dynamo, gearing, and belts, it may be assumed that a dynamo of 100-watts output would be the right machine for the available power. The voltage chosen might well be 25, this being its lowest rate at normal speed, which may be assumed at 1500 revs. per minute.

Under these circumstances, and assuming

pulley A (fig. 75) to run at 200 revs. per minute (by whatever gearing used), A might be 12
inches diameter × 2 inches width; B, 6 inches ×

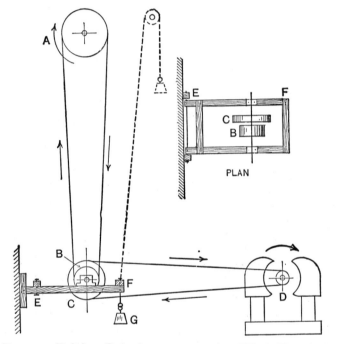

FIG. 75.—Driving Belt Arrangement for Wind Electrical
Plant.

3; C, 8 inches × 2; and D, the dynamo pulley,
2 inches × 2 inches. This gives a rather higher
ratio than is required—an error on the right
side. The belt between A and B should be 1½
inches × ³⁄₁₆ inch, the pulleys being about 6 feet
centres, and belt CD 1 inch wide × ⅛ inch thick,
also with about 6 feet drive.

There would be twelve accumulator cells, each of from 150 to 200 ampere-hour capacity, which would be easily capable of dealing with the full current for twenty-four hours' continuous charging. The capacity mentioned is the maximum suitable for the given plant, but the minimum may be anything down to twelve pocket-batteries, if so desired. Within the iimits given, the greater the capacity the more the independence of conditions of wind.

With regard to the automatic switch, a little experimenting and adjusting will be needed to ensure its correct working. The electro-magnets may be two ordinary bell-magnets, wound with No. 36 wire, the bobbins being about $1\frac{1}{4}$ inches long and 1 inch diameter outside. A resistance may be needed in series with this winding, or the effect may be tried of connecting up only six of the cells to these coils, the six on the left-hand side in fig. 73 being, of course, selected. All four bobbins will be joined in series. Over the fine wire on each bobbin will be wound from six to twelve turns (to be determined by experiment) of No. 16 or 14 gauge cotton-covered wire, the winding being in same direction as the fine wire in each case, so that the current is a reinforcing one when being supplied from the dynamo. The balance of the permanent magnet can be adjusted by moving the copper rod CR either to right or left.

The output from such an installation may of

course be anything up to the safe discharge rate of the battery employed. Assuming the normal conditions of charging to be, say, 100 watts for ten hours (equal to 1000 watt-hours), and that this charge is to be used in two evenings, there would be available 500 watt-hours per evening, less the losses in transforming, or, say, 80 watts for five hours. Fortunately at the time of year —winter—when longer lighting is necessary more wind-power is also available. Of course, only metallic-filament lamps should be used, when it will be seen that with proper proportioning of the plant quite a respectable output in light is to be obtained. The lamps for the above installation would be 16 volt.

If the loan of an anemometer cannot be obtained, a simple form of wind-pressure meter should be used to determine the right weight (R, fig. 49) required to just hold the windmill sails at the velocity decided upon. Such an apparatus is sketched in fig. 76. It is merely a sheet of stout cardboard, 2 feet $\times$ 1 foot, hung on one of the narrow edges by a hinge of linen, the middle of the lower edge being connected as shown to a small spring letter balance capable of reading up to at least one pound. A table of wind-pressures and velocities is given below, by which any pressure registered can be converted into velocity. The pressure-board must, of course, squarely face the wind blowing at the time of the experiment. Note that the spring

balance is just at zero when no wind is im-
pressed on the board, or a false reading may
be obtained. If made to the given sizes, the

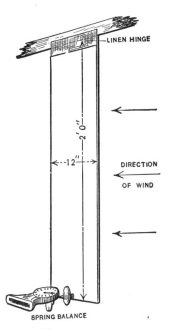

FIG. 76.—A Simple Wind-pressure Gauge.

readings will be direct measurements of the
pressure per square foot.

The brake horse-power of a windmill can be
taken in exactly the same way as that of a
steam-engine, the only difficulty being the usual
unsteadiness of the wind. At a time when the
wind is fairly steady and about right in velocity,

such a test should be made, one observer watching the pressure-meter and noting the pressure, say, every half-minute, another reading the spring balance of the brake at similar intervals, the test lasting for a quarter of an hour. Average results may then be obtained, which may be extremely useful for determining the size of dynamo required, it being remembered that the power of the wind varies (theoretically) directly as the cube of its velocity. In practice the variation rate lies between this and the *square* of the velocity.

TABLE OF WIND PRESSURE AND VELOCITIES.

Miles per hour.	Feet per minute.	Feet per second.	Force in lbs. per sq. foot.	Description.
1	88	1.47	.005	Hardly perceptible.
2	176	2.93	.020	Just perceptible.
3	264	4.4	.044	
4	352	5.87	.079	Gentle breeze.
5	440	7.33	.123	
10	880	14.67	.492	Pleasant breeze.
15	1320	22	1.107	
20	1760	29.3	1.968	Brisk gale.
25	2200	36.6	3.075	
30	2640	44	4.428	High wind.
35	3080	51.3	6.027	
40	3520	58.6	7.872	Very high wind.
45	3960	66	9.963	
50	4400	73.3	12.300	Storm.
ᴜ0	5280	88	17.712	Great storm.
70	6160	102.7	24.108	
80	7040	117.3	31.488	Hurricane.
100	8800	146.6	49.200	